E. P. Papanoutsos.

JOHN ANTON

Critical Humanism as a Philosophy of Culture:
The Case of E. P. Papanoutsos

A TALK

EDITED AND WITH AN INTRODUCTION BY
Theofanis G. Stavrou

The Third Annual Public Lecture
in Modern Greek Studies
Special Collections
University of Minnesota Libraries
Minneapolis

The North Central Publishing Company
1981

Library of Congress Card Number: 81-81840

ISBN 0-935476-07-5

The publication of this volume was made possible with assistance from the Graduate School, College of Liberal Arts, University of Minnesota, and from Nostos, the Society for the Study of Greek Life and Thought, Minneapolis, Minnesota.

TABLE OF CONTENTS

INTRODUCTION *

"It is man's world of the mind that I endeavor to investigate, his Art, his Ethics, his Science that I seek to analyse and to understand." With this statement, Evangelos P. Papanoutsos, a leading modern Greek thinker, summarized his intellectual pilgrimage which began with a desire to study "Metaphysics" and ended by studying what amounted to a kind of "Anthropology," a transition dictated perhaps as much by historical circumstances as by personal inclination. Frequently young nation-states such as modern Greece view their men of letters as enlighteners or commentators on political, social and cultural questions, as educators and reform-

---

*This introductory essay appeared originally as the text to an illustrated brochure, *Evangelos P. Papanoutsos, Philosopher, Educator, Critic*, which was published under the auspices of the Modern Greek Collection, Special Collections, University of Minnesota Libraries, in connection with the Third Annual Celebration of Modern Greek Letters honoring E. P. Papanoutsos. The event took place on May 16, 1980, under the sponsorship of Special Collections, the History Department and several other units and programs: Concerts and lectures, Humanities, Classics, Slavic and East European Studies, the School of Education, and with support from the Kostas and Eleni Ouranis Foundation, Athens, Greece. The event followed the pattern of the two previous occasions when the focus was on Nikos Kazantzakis (1978) and Pandelis Prevelakis (1979).

Speakers for the occasion included Professor Theofanis G. Stavrou who gave a brief report on the progress of modern Greek studies at the University of Minnesota, and Mr. Austin McLean, Chief of Special Collections, who commented on the progress in developing the Modern Greek Collection. Professor Stavrou also acted as Master of Ceremonies and introduced the other speakers beginning with Professor Fred Lukermann, Dean of the College of Liberal Arts, who emphasized the significance of modern Greek studies at this University, and the Honorable Spyridon Dokianos, Greek Consul General from Chicago who officially represented the Greek State. The featured speakers were Professor Robert Beck who spoke on "Papanoutsos and Education" with emphasis on the 'need and role of vision,' and Professor John P. Anton who spoke on "Critical Humanism and the Philosophy of Culture: The Case of E. P. Papanoutsos."

The event was supplemented by an elegant exhibit consisting of approximately 115 items — books and magazines, manuscripts, correspondence, photographs, diagrams and works of art. Central to the exhibit, which remained open until July 31, was the creative work of E. P. Papanoutsos representing six decades of literary

1

ers, as well as preservers and transmitters of the cultural heritage. The intellectual and cultural history of modern Greece attests to the central role its men of letters have played and continue to play in various manifestations of the national experience. Whether residing within the boundaries of the modern Greek state or in the diaspora, most Greek intellectuals inevitably attempt to define or redefine the status, dilemmas and prospects of neohellenism in its national and international context. They do so with varying degrees of dedication and success, but the general impact of their efforts and the tradition they create underscores the basic premise from which they presumably operate: an unexamined life, individual or national, is not worth living. In short, consciously or unconsciously, they become critics, conservative or progressive.

The life and work of Evangelos P. Papanoutsos is an intricate part of twentieth-century Greek history and culture. Himself as old as the century (he was born in 1900 in Pireas), Papanoutsos has been a careful student and observer of the modern Greek scene, enriching it with his varied activities. He has expressed his concerns and hopes in over forty major works, philosophical and educational treatises, and scores of critical articles in newspapers and scholarly journals in Greece and abroad. Gradually, he emerged as one of the country's leading philosophers, educators and cultural critics. Well versed in the classics and always appreciative of the classical heritage, he nevertheless remained obsessively fascinated by the challenges facing modern man and the latter's responses to them. This fascination left its indelible mark on the life and work of E. P. Papanoutsos.

After graduation from the Gymnasium in Pireas, Papanoutsos studied theology and philosophy at the University of Athens (1915–1919), and like other ambitious Greek students of his generation who wished to excel in philosophical studies, he left for

---

activity and involvement in the question of modern Greek education, as well as commentaries on his life and work.

Two additional items of information — one biographical, the other bibliographical — should be of interest to readers of this volume as well as those who attended the May 16, 1980 event honoring E. P. Papanoutsos. On February 13, 1981, the Academy of Athens elected him as a regular member to that body, recognizing in this way his manifold contributions to modern Greek culture. Equally important is the special volume devoted to the life and work of Papanoutsos scheduled to appear this spring as No. 13 of *Tetradhia Efthinis* (Athens: Ekdhoseis ton Philon) and a biography of Papanoutsos by G. P. Henderson, University of Dundee, Scotland, scheduled to be published by G. K. Hall in the Twayne World Authors Series in 1982. These volumes will certainly contribute toward a more systematic study of E. P. Papanoutsos and his work, and of modern Greek education.

2

Europe at the first opportunity. He studied philosophy and education at the Universities of Berlin, Tübingen and Paris (1924–26),
where among other things he familiarized himself with the contemporary philosophical currents in Europe and America. He received his Doctor of Philosophy degree from the University of
Tübingen in 1927 with a dissertation on *The Religious Experience
in Plato*. Written and defended in German, the dissertation was
published in Alexandria, Egypt, where Papanoutsos had moved
soon after his graduation from the University of Athens in 1919.

The Egyptian sojourn, which with the exception of the few
years when he studied in Europe, lasted until 1931, and was
probably the most crucial landmark in the intellectual and cultural growth of Papanoutsos. Infinitely more cosmopolitan than
Athens, Alexandria then claimed a thriving Greek community
with its own schools, newspapers, publishing industry and literary circles. There Papanoutsos began his life-long involvement
with Greek education as a teacher at the Averoff Greek Gymnasium, where he tried to introduce some of the new pedagogical
techniques he had studied in Europe. There he began studying
French, German and English, and there he became friends with a
select group of men of letters of the Greek diaspora, including
Constantine Cavafy and Glafkos Alithersis, whom Papanoutsos
describes as his intellectual mentors in the early stages of his
career. Finally, in Alexandria he published his first philosophical
works. For the rest of his life, as philosopher, educator and critic,
Papanoutsos labored to complete the edifice whose foundations,
in a way, he laid in Alexandria.

Preoccupation with philosophical questions accounts for a
major part of Papanoutsos' creative activity. At one time he identified this preoccupation as the major labor, purpose and joy of his
life. It started in Alexandria in 1921 when as a young intellectual
he wrote an extensive critical review (seventy-six printed pages) of
a book written by a local Greek physician entitled *Responsibility
and Freedom*, a book which defended scientific positivism and a
monistic materialism. As early as then Papanoutsos pointed out
that man's "spiritual world" — the domains of beauty, goodness
and truth — has its own structure and requires a special method
for its proper investigation, understanding and appraisal. He pursued this philosophical approach systematically for the rest of his
life. His first step in this venture was the publication in 1928 of
The Trilogy of the Mind: Art, Ethics, Science, in which he outlined
the main ideas and principles of his project. These ideas were
further developed in respective volumes during the following
decade: *About Art* (1930); *About Ethics* (1932); and *About Science*

3

(1937). But it took another fifteen years (1938–1953) of hard and systematic work before the project resulted in the publication of the three huge volumes under the general title *The World of the Mind*; vol. I, *Aesthetics* (1948); vol. II, *Ethics* (1949); and vol. III, *Gnosiology* (1954); totaling 1,352 pages. The third volume was translated into English as *The Foundations of Knowledge* (1968). This was the first successful attempt by a modern Greek at a systematic philosophy in which the principal philosophical problems are rigorously examined, revealing simultaneously the author's mastery of European philosophy and his own originality. Despite its size, *The World of the Mind* enjoyed phenomenal commercial success, by Greek standards, each volume having gone through several editions. In the meantime, supplementary essays on the philosophy of art, written after the first edition of his *Aesthetics*, appeared in separate volumes: *Philosophy and Paideia* (1958), *Philosophical Problems* (1964), and *Logos and Man* (1971). It seemed as if the completion of *The World of the Mind* liberated its author who subsequently proceeded with alarming regularity to flood the Greek bookstores with volumes of philosophical content. In addition to the above, the most significant were *La Catharsis des passions d'après Aristote* (1953), *Psychology* (1970), *Logic* (1970), *Practical Philosophy* (1973), *Law and Virtue* (1974), *The Right of Force* (1976), *State and Justice* (1976), and *The Crisis of Our Civilization* (1978). Parallel with these activities, Papanoutsos translated into Greek, with analytical introductions and comments, Immanuel Kant's *Essays* (1971), and David Hume's *Essays: Philosophy, Ethics, and Politics* (1974), as well as Hume's *Essays: Economics, History and Sociopolitics* (1979). Papanoutsos had, of course, earlier engaged himself with Kant's and Hume's thought while working on his *The World of the Mind*, and especially in his *Philosophy and Paideia* where he dealt with the problem of the "Meaning of History," but he wanted to make these works more readily accessible to the Greek reading public. In fact, his translation of Hume was the first such undertaking in Greek. Finally, reference should be made to the two-volume edition of *Modern Greek Philosophy* (1953, 1956), which is a useful guide to the contributions of modern Greek thinkers from the seventeenth to the twentieth centuries. With this work Papanoutsos sought to encourage the study of this neglected aspect of the intellectual and cultural history of modern Greece.

Papanoutsos' success as a philosophical writer stems chiefly from his commitment to the field, his clarity of thought, and above all his clarity of expression. With the exception of his first philosophical essays, he deliberately wrote entirely in the demotic

4

of which he became an ardent champion. He maintained that the demotic could and should express with precision and ease the most complicated philosophical ideas, and his own writings certainly verify that. In this respect one could claim that Papanoutsos vindicated the demotic language in the philosophical expression, just as Palamas had done earlier in the poetic expression. In any case, with a handful of his contemporaries, some of whom belonged to academic circles, Papanoutsos contributed significantly to the creation of what can be described as a "popular" philosophical climate in Greece. Commercial publishers assumed the responsibility to publish philosophical works which the public welcomed, and Papanoutsos was delighted with the realization that his generation had learned to write and to study philosophy and not only the history of philosophy.

If philosophy was Papanoutsos' great joy, education was his great yearning, his life's great concern. Papanoutsos' formal training and his own philosophical inquiries led him from the beginning to the related question of *paideia* or education in the broad sense of the word; that is to say, the process by which man develops his sense of judgment and perspective and which also serves as a link between thought and social action. As early as 1924, he published his *Pragmatism or Humanism: Elaboration and Criticism of the Theories of a Great Current of Contemporary Philosophy*, which concentrates primarily on pragmatism as this had been shaped by Peirce, Dewey, Schiller, and James. Papanoutsos maintained his interest in pragmatism throughout his life, and he became an advocate of educational reforms which would correspond with social and economic realities and the introduction of pedagogical methods which would facilitate and make learning meaningful. In short, he rebelled against scholasticism which characterized the entire Greek educational system and which failed to meet the nation's needs. Gradually, he became a follower of the ideas of the short-lived Educational Society, founded in 1911 by A. Delmouzos, which constituted the first real attempt at educational reforms in Greece.

As a philosopher, educator and responsible citizen, Papanoutsos could not envisage national progress without a progressive and imaginative educational system, and the latter was inconceivable without major educational reforms. Upon his return to Greece from Alexandria in 1931, he became increasingly involved in that country's most controversial debate and the politics of education, which were hopelessly and treacherously confused by association with political ideologies, ranging from the extreme right to the extreme left, with liberal educators such as Papanoutsos caught

5

repeatedly in an uncomfortable squeeze. But his ideas as an educator were gaining ground and between 1931 and 1944 he became successively founder and/or director of teachers training schools and of pedagogical academies in various parts of Greece, such as Mytilini, Alexandroupoli, Yannina, Tripoli and Pireas. Intermittently, between 1944 and 1965 he served as General Director and General Secretary of the Ministry of Education, usually during the period when George Papandreou commanded political power. Few can match his dedication to and struggle for educational reforms. Undaunted by political opposition, including the Greek military regime (1967–1974), Papanoutsos persisted until he witnessed the enforcement of educational reforms, first in 1964 and then in 1976. It was partly his desire to act as a watchdog of the educational reforms process that he served as a member of the Greek Parliament (representing the Democratic Center) for the period 1974–1977.

Central to Papanoutsos' educational reform program was his determination to implement the demotic as the language of instruction. It was another expression of his loyalty to the language of the people and his conviction that the use of the *Katharevousa* in Greek schools had already done irreparable damage/to the nation. Much to his satisfaction, the 1976 reform initiated the demotic as the language of instruction at all levels of education. But the road to 1976 was a hard one. Until then the ideal of educational reform had been sustained by Herculean efforts in other spheres of activity. It was necessary to educate the politicians and the educators, as well as the public, about the crucial importance of the reforms. This Papanoutsos sought to accomplish through the publication of a monthly educational journal, *Paideia* (later *Paideia kai Zoe*), which he managed almost singlehandedly from 1946 to 1961. The publication of this journal alone could easily earn for Papanoutsos a major place in modern Greek letters. That was only the beginning. In 1946 he undertook the responsibility to write a weekly column for the leading Athenian newspaper, *To Vima*, a column which he wrote until 1967. A selection of these articles appeared in book form under the titles *Ephemera* (1950) and *Timely and Untimely* (1962). In 1965 on the morrow of the first victory of the reforms, he published his *Struggles and Agonies for Paideia*, a landmark in the educational history of Greece. This work was later supplemented by his *Paideia, Our Great Problem*, published in 1976, the year of the implementation of the Educational Reform. While promoting reforms, Papanoutsos organized and directed the Technical and Professional Schools of the Athenian Technological Institute (1958–1975), a program which reflected his commitment to technical education, and his conviction that the educational process should transform itself into social action.

For political and personal reasons, Papanoutsos never held a position at a Greek university. In the long run this proved to be a blessing for he was able to devote more time to his scholarly and creative work. But he loved teaching, that is to say, to share his ideas with students and friends, and to this day nothing gives him greater pleasure than when he is viewed as a teacher. With the help of friends who shared similar convictions, Papanoutsos embarked upon one of the most creative and successful educational experiments in modern Greece and possibly anywhere in the world. Soon after the Second World War, they founded the cultural society, *Athenaion*, which was a free university offering the public in the evening free lessons at the university level. Papanoutsos assumed responsibility for supervising the "curriculum offerings," and soon it became one of the most heavily attended educational programs in Greece. One of the remarkable characteristics of this venture was that its curriculum included courses in the humanities and the sciences, and that it became a forum for the ideas of younger as well as older Greek intellectuals.

An examination of the society's report on the first twenty years of its accomplishments (1946–1966) reveals the most impressive array of activities, courses, lectures and excursions providing excellent instruction in Greek history and culture. The list of participating professors reads like a *Who's Who* of the best teachers and most exciting intellectuals of the period. Many scholarly books which appeared during this time in Greece were first discussed, or the subject matter first taught, in the halls of the *Athenaion*. Papanoutsos himself gave a series of courses on philosophy, including one on modern Greek philosophy.

All these efforts culminated in the 1976 Educational Reform. And quite appropriately when soon thereafter Papanoutsos was asked to contribute the first volume to a series of modern Greek biographies, under the auspices of the National Bank Cultural Foundation of Greece, he chose as his subject A. Delmouzos, the initiator of "educational demoticism," who earlier had served as an inspiration for him.

As a cultural critic, Papanoutsos also displayed a lively interest in modern Greek literature. He knew personally most of the major Greek writers of his generation, such as Cavafy, Kazantzakis, Palamas, Prevelakis, and Sikelianos, and he contributed to the leading Greek literary journals. As in the case of his philosophical and educational concerns, the language consideration — the use of the demotic — was again central. He therefore felt a special admiration for and affinity with the champions of literary demoticism. In 1949, Papanoutsos published in book form three useful studies on three major Greek poets, Palamas, Cavafy, and Sikelianos, which had appeared earlier in literary journals. Like many other works of Papanoutsos it, too, went through several editions and received the endorsement of some leading critics, even though many others were scandalized by his study of Cavafy whom he called "didactic." In reality, it is a subtle appreciation of the Alexandrian poet from a philosophical thinker's perspective and a study which could serve well many Cavafy students. Papanoutsos was also interested in the history of modern Greek criticism. In collaboration with I. M. Panayotopoulos and Dion. Zakythinos, he prepared a special volume on the subject *Modern Greek Criticism* in the Basic Library series (1956). As is the case with the two volumes on modern Greek philosophy in the same series, the collaborators direct their attention to the history and state of the art of modern Greek criticism, especially the nineteenth and twentieth centuries. And needless to say, Papanoutsos' critical comments on several works of literature and art are also scattered throughout his numerous articles, many of which first appeared in his weekly column in *To Vima*. Finally, he displayed his critical acumen as supervisor and collaborator of two of the most ambitious publishing ventures in Greece: the publication of the 100-volumes of ancient writers with modern Greek translation (1948–1958); and the 48-volume Basic Library series (1950–1960), an essential tool for the students of neohellenism.

This year (July 27, 1980), Evangelos P. Papanoutsos celebrates his eightieth birthday. He has generously fulfilled his role as a man of letters in a young and maturing nation-state. He presently lives alone (his wife Julia, a self-taught painter, died in 1972) in his Athens apartment on Anagnostopoulou 10, where he enjoys a view of the Acropolis. There he receives scholars and friends, Greeks and non-Greeks, with whom he discusses eagerly topics ranging from the philosophy and politics of Greek education to international issues. For his numerous contributions to philosophy, education, and humanistic studies, the University of St. Andrews in Scotland conferred on him an honorary doctorate in 1965. In 1977 the Society of Modern Greek Writers elected him as Honorary President.

This Third Annual Celebration of Greek Letters at the University of Minnesota is a tribute to Evangelos Papanoutsos, the philosopher, the critic, and above all the teacher. In 1966 while on a special educational tour in the United States, Papanoutsos visited Minnesota briefly and recorded his impressions in his book *America: A Chapter in the History of Man* (1966). Since then he has maintained contact with colleagues and friends at the University of Minnesota, and has always been ready to render his assistance in the common venture for *paideia*.

As is the custom, this celebration is accompanied by an exhibit of Papanoutsos' published works, as well as many unpublished manuscripts, correspondence, and other documents reflecting the range of his activities, and supplemented by commentaries on the life and work of Papanoutsos written by Greek and non-Greek scholars. We are especially pleased to display a copy of Mr. Papanoutsos' unpublished memoirs that he donated to the University of Minnesota Library, which is a valuable document not only on the life of its author but also on the intellectual and cultural history of modern Greece. The Papanoutsos collection will serve as the basis for developing the Modern Greek Collection in the fields of education and philosophy. In many respects this is the finest tribute one could pay to this prolific writer, cultural critic and bold educator. He summarized many of his struggles and agonies when he stated that his great objective was to teach his fellow Greeks that "the Christian may hold the Old Testament with one hand and Plato and Aristotle with the other without fear that his faith will be distorted and without hating his educators," a succinct description of the universal problem of conflict and reconciliation in the educational process. Finally, this celebration is in keeping with our efforts at Minnesota to improve systematically the Modern Greek Collection and course offerings in modern Greek history and culture. This, too, is a tribute to Evangelos P. Papanoutsos and his commitment to *paideia* and whose life and work was a personification of what the Greeks would call the joy of learning.

Theofanis G. Stavrou
University of Minnesota
May 15, 1981

CRITICAL HUMANISM
AS A PHILOSOPHY OF CULTURE:
THE CASE OF E. P. PAPANOUTSOS*

I. The Man and His Works

In order to introduce the theme of this lecture, there is really no need to repeat here what I have already published elsewhere.[1] However, it will help my purposes if in my effort to highlight certain aspects of Papanoutsos' philosophy, I may use this opportunity to sketch briefly the main phases of his career as a teacher, thinker and writer. His philosophical writings fall into four more or less distinct periods. The first period covers his two dissertations and related writings, from 1921 to 1928. We know that he wrote one dissertation for his doctorate at the University of Tübingen which had the title *The Religious Experience in Plato*[2] *(Das Religiöse Erleben bei Platon)*, and one which he submitted to the Faculty of Philosophy at the University of Athens. In the latter he sought to defend on rational grounds the religious philosophy of Christianity, but after he developed certain doubts about the soundness of his argument he decided to withdraw the dissertation. He had in the meantime become attracted to the issues which the growing literature of Anglo-American pragmatism had formulated. He tried his hand in this area, and wrote a detailed analysis of the claims for a sound humanism which pragmatism was making. The result was his book, *Pragmatism or Humanism*,

---

*This is a revised version of the talk Professor John Anton gave at Minnesota on the occasion of the event honoring E. P. Papanoutsos. All translations of passages from the writings of E. P. Papanoutsos cited in this essay are by Professor Anton. In the text of the introduction, this essay and its notes, only the English titles of the works of Papanoutsos are cited. For a list of Papanoutsos' works in their Greek as well as corresponding English titles, consult the bibliographic supplement at the end of this volume. Editor's note.
[1] Evangelos P. Papanoutsos, *The Foundations of Knowledge*, edited and with an Introduction by John P. Anton, translated by Basil Coukis and John P. Anton (Albany: State University of New York Press, 1968). See pp. ix–xxx.
[2] Translated by Papanoutsos himself into Greek and published in 1971.

published in 1924. Dominant during this period was the determination to come to grips with the persistent problem of how to reconcile the ideas which the Classical and the Christian traditions had contributed to the mainstream of the Western Mind.

The second phase, from 1928 to 1937, is a period of programmatic investigations probing into the difficulties attending the theories which defended the reducibility of method in value theory to that of the natural sciences. He argued his position first in his *Pragmatism or Humanism* and then decided to extend it more systematically in his three-volume work, *The Trilogy of the Mind*. The third phase falls roughly between 1948 and 1954. It reflects his extraordinary productivity, especially with the writing of three larger works, all of which undertake to define and refine the philosophical method for the critical examination of the creative role of consciousness in the scientific knowledge, the artistic achievement and ethical conduct. The outcome was a monumental three-volume work under the general title "The World of the Mind", consisting of three distinct works, *Aesthetics* (1948), *Ethics* (1949) and *Gnosiologia* (1954). The fourth phase began after 1954, when Papanoutsos started working on particular problems in various philosophical fields, practical affairs and topics in literature and education. In the publications of this period he shared with his readers the results of inquiries he undertook by applying his critical conception of method. He was determined to penetrate even deeper into all the vital issues of cultural life that had already come within his purview.

On the whole there are three constant themes running through his major writings: (i) the activities which constitute "the world of the mind" as these find fulfillment in science, art and morality. They are identified as the theoretical, the practical and the aesthetic expressions of humanity, and together comprise a world emerging with its own laws, forms, demands and standards. Papanoutsos considers it fundamental to his thesis that the effected world of the mind requires a *sui generis* set of procedures for its understanding, exploration and description. The story of the projection, discovery and elucidation of these emergent areas of the world of the mind is the record of human consciousness, and the continuous cultivation and the deliberate effort to perfect each of them, education at its best. (ii) The other constant theme is that creative activity cannot be reduced to the status of a biochemical process or a phenomenon to be subsumed under events ordinarily explainable through socio-historical determinations alone. Creativity, for Papanoutsos, has its own telic structure, its own rationale, and constitutes a special mode of being. When seen for what it is in its essential character it manifests itself as being at once autonomous and individual. (iii) With equal steadfastedness he endeavored to show that freedom (and the concomitant concept of responsibility) belongs to a sphere of its own and hence falls outside the orbit of the phenomena which require the idea of causality for their understanding. Papanoutsos regards freedom as an ultimate condition and also the generative source of all significant human action.[3] As it turns out, he takes the view that it is impossible to assign meaning to the concept of culture without prior recognition, in some identifiable and practical way, of freedom as an ultimate condition.

There is hardly an "Introduction" to any of his works in which he does not draw the reader's attention to the concept of method. All his themes and problems, reflections and investigations, he tells us, are best understood when together with the dialectic of the argument the reader keeps a vigilant eye on the traditions and historical developments that figure in the background as generative forces. As cultural beings, he believes, we all have our roots in certain traditions, particularly in those we deliberately set out to master and extend. Papanoutsos' own are to be found in the two great Enlightenment periods of Western Civilization, the more recent one of the eighteenth century, which philosophers in particular readily associate with the names of Hume and Kant, and the more remote one, the Greek Enlightenment of the Fifth Century B.C., which the great Sophists, Socrates and his companions ushered into history.[4]

The two Enlightenments provided two distinct models which his own philosophical work was to explore and emulate. However the substantive problems he discussed sprang from the realities of the twentieth century: the agonies of the contemporary world and the sufferings of his own people. The ecumenical and the ethnic sides of his personality intertwine at every juncture of his career as

---

[3] His first publication appeared when he was only twenty-one and was titled *The Problem of the Freedom of the Will* (1921). It was an attempt to argue against the current reductionist positions and the deterministic philosophy of physicalism. Sixty years later and less puzzled by the problem which marked the beginning of his inquiries, Papanoutsos remains the staunch defender of human freedom he always was. The change that has taken place since his 1921 essay can be seen as a gradual shift of interest from a preoccupation with the metaphysics of morals to a more direct analysis of freedom in concrete contexts. See *Ethics* (1949), Ch. II, pp. 205–18; Ch. III, section 3, pp. 253–93; esp. Ch. V, section 1, pp. 371–88; also, *Philosophy and Paideia* (1958), Ch. I, "The Problem of Freedom," pp. 9–80. For discussions on special problems see *Philosophical Problems* (1963), Part II, pp. 103–44; *Logos and Man* (1971), Part I, pp. 19–126. A brief summary of his main thesis is given in *The Crisis of Our Civilization* (1978), pp. 266–71.

[4] Comp. *Philosophy and Paideia* (1958), pp. 218–35; also *Philosophical Problems* (1963), Part III, Ch. 4, "The Philosophical Aspect of the History of Philosophy," pp. 179–215; *The Crisis of Our Civilization* (1978), pp. 51–56.

educator and philosophical statesman. As educator he defended in practice as well as in theory the view that the goals of education can neither be clarified nor properly understood outside of a carefully delineated critical philosophy of culture. This extraordinarily difficult task calls for an enlightened outlook which also defines the ethos of the critical philosopher. This cannot be other than that of the humanist. If we agree with Papanoutsos that the responsible life of the individual is also the life of freedom as affirmation and critique of ideals, the question that needs to be asked is why his work falls short of constructing a comprehensive political theory, and one that could suggest the way out of the contemporary crisis. It is this crucial question that the present essay considers to be the issue and the challenge. It is the very question that loomed largely in the minds of the philosophers whose own thinking brought about the two Enlightenments Papanoutsos regards as the high moments of Western culture.

II. The Concept of Humanity

To the perennial question "What is it to be human?" Papanoutsos after a studious survey of the history of the quest, settled for the following: "Man is the unique being in the universe who has the inalienable right to be treated always as an end, never as a means." [5] It is a formulation very much close to Kant's own, and proposed on the ground that it has none of the shortcomings so many other definitions in the history of the concept have exhibited under close scrutiny. It is instructive to follow Papanoutsos' meticulous analyses of the diverse treatments of the concept of humanity and the changes it has undergone during certain crucial phases of history when the concept was deliberately tied mainly to the artistic and literary monuments of the age. Thus the crystallization of the concept of humanity as end and measure of all values and as carrying with it the demand for the preservation of human dignity under all circumstances, he recognized as marking the greatest gain in our cultural history. It took the labor of innumerable generations and the passage of many civilizations before human thought could state this concept with the clarity and depth in which we view it today.

Authentic humanism underscores the irreplaceable significance of each human being, and thus recommends itself as the source of a practical principle from which we derive the guidelines for all moral and political action. Any plan, decision or thought that in any form or fashion violates this commitment not only com-

---

[5] *The Crisis of Our Civilization* (1978), p. 222; for a brief but succinct discussion on "The Definition of Man," pp. 218–23.

14

promises the concept of humanity, and as such should be regarded the worst of all crimes, but also has the devastating effect of allowing for habits that unavoidably lead to self-degrading acts. Authentic humanism, as Papanoutsos understands it, also provides the foundations on which to build a sound philosophy of education. Thus educating and meeting the demands for enlightened acculturation are processes that depend for their success on our ability to determine the means and correlate them to the ends which secure the consummate goal of becoming fully human. But ensuring ethical fulfillment, in the sense that every human being is entitled to be complete, independent and free, requires making available to the members of every community the means that provide for the preservation of body and the ennoblement of mind, from food, shelter and health,[6] to science, art and justice.

If authentic humanism is the best protection we have to warn us against self-degrading habits then the chief corrolary of the idea of humanity is a theory of action which remains unswervingly devoted to *philanthropia*, love of mankind as both ennobled feeling and practical ethics. We owe the first formulation of this idea to classical Greece, although it has parallels as a concern in other traditions, and the Biblical texts in particular.[7] Be that as it may, we find that the early elucidations of the Greeks had assigned to the idea meanings associated with such basic values as honor, respect and trust, all of which were joined together with the bonds of solidarity and justice. It was recognition of the common fate and the common nature of all human beings that set the Greeks on the path to discover those eternal verities which prevail in the end and assign value to all the great moments as well as the minor episodes of humanity. When dramatists of the stature of Aeschylus, Sophocles and Euripides, and brilliant philosophers like Plato and Aristotle, paid tribute to the greatness of which human beings are capable of attaining, stating it through insight, argument and observation, or presenting it by way of mimesis and

---

[6] *Struggles and Agonies for Paideia* (1965), 280–81.

[7] *Ibid.*, and especially the essay titled "Humanism" pp. 259–63. He notes there: "This certainly does not mean that prior to the Greeks 'history' had not yet discovered human awareness and the problem of man. To insist on such a view is to say that all 'history' has its beginning in ancient Greece, a view far from being true. However, the fact remains that never before that time did human existence as a life form and as moral value project itself to be cognized in self-awareness and with explicit self-pride as it did with the civilization of the ancient Greeks. It was during this period that the idea of humanity reached its apogee by manifesting itself prominently in all walks of life. It is expressed in their political life as the concept of democracy; in their poetry, as the concept of tragedy; and in their reflective life, as the concept of philosophy." (p. 259).

15

reenactment on the stage, they expressed more than their confidence in the power of man to overcome evil. They also declared their faith in the ultimate triumph of justice in human affairs.

As Papanoutsos repeatedly points out, the Hellenic conception of "love of mankind," despite its many common and overlapping points with that of Christian love, is shown to be less charitable. The latter has the advantage of having given prominence to the communicable emotion of co-suffering. The two ways of understanding *philanthropia* receive their most successful integration in the ethical philosophy of Immanuel Kant, summarized in the ethical imperative which states that human beings be always treated as ends in themselves and never as means. Here the universal love of Christian fellowship, the maxim "love thy neighbor," blends harmoniously with the classical view of humanity with its emphasis on honor and dignity, and both fit well within the universal framework of the Stoic vision of cosmopolitanism. [8] It is to this refined version of the Enlightment view of man that we still turn in search for the moral foundations on which to build a philosophy of education. Against this rich background of philosophical traditions Papanoutsos sought to establish the ethics of his critical humanism. It is a perspective that enables him to identify and all those cases of man's inhumanity to man which taken together form the contours and the deadening predicaments of our cultural crisis.

Three special cases loom largely in the background of Papanoutsos' protest against the abuse of human potential and mocking of the idea of freedom. He is particularly sensitive to the destructive consequences such actions have for those groups or individuals who because of their circumstances cannot defend and protect themselves. Recent history has provided ample evidence from which to illustrate all three cases. [9] First, there is the *de facto* abuse of the unchecked power the larger nations have at their

---

[8] *Ibid.*, p. 262.

[9] Papanoutsos' reflections on the broader issues generated by "man's inhumanity to man" after two world wars, were stated in an article he published in the journal he was editing at the time (1954), *Paideia and Life* (from 1946 to 1961); it was reprinted as the leading article titled "Outlines of a Program," in his *Struggles and Agonies for Paideia* (1965). It was written in response to a questionnaire a weekly newspaper had sent to Greece's leading statesmen and intellectuals on the post-war problems touching on the survival of the nation, asking what values should be emphasized to quicken the recovery and re-focus the national aims of public education. Commenting on the demands the situation was making on those who had been trusted with the nation's destiny, Papanoutsos drew attention to the wide-spread fear about the uncertainties that haunted the smaller nations. This fear, he declared, was due to a number of factors that in the long run could pose a real threat and to the point of rendering the small and defenseless nations an endangered species.

disposal and the advantages this power affords them to impose their will on others without fear of consequences. Such abuses have been frequent and have set in motion the forces that make the assimilation or absorption of smaller nations to the more powerful ones almost inevitable. The threat does not stop with the prospect of territorial and political annexation: it carries with it the gradual effacement of the respective cultures along with the languages, literatures and social experiences rooted in venerable traditions to which even the super-powers owe an historical debt. Processes of this sort have the painful and insidious effect of profoundly altering the ethnic dimensions of personalities by flattening them into an unwanted and perturbing psychological otherness. Secondly, the smaller nations, because of their inferior military technology, are subject to being reduced to the unfortunate positive of having to face the possible fate of total annihilation in the event of a thermonuclear war between the super-powers. It is the misfortune of the innocent to suffer what they must. Thirdly, there is the increasing danger of the gradual and planned manipulation of the political institutions which set in motion the processes that can easily lead to depersonalization. The super-powers do more than force disruptive changes upon their own constituencies. Unfortunately, they have ample resources to influence and impose them also on those of the smaller nations. The latter lack the requisite resources to fight the gigantic waves of social transformation that affect the quality of life in the advanced technocratic societies.[10] Once these processes are well

---

[10] In a brief essay titled "Types of Freedom," Papanoutsos examines what it means to be free, and correlates the diverse conditions of life to the validity of the claims we make to being free while living in situations that fail to satisfy the following canon: "Having one's own will and acting according to one's own will." The question thus is: How do we know we are authentically free rather than believing we are free while acting under pressure, either due to ignorance, previous conditioning, or some other external factor not of our own choosing and without our reasoned consent? The problem here is where to draw the line between genuinely autonomous and heteronomous conduct. If the latter does not differ from slavery, there is still the question whether it is possible for someone who is involuntarily a slave to be in some real sense free. It makes sense, Papanoutsos argues, to speak about a "freedom" ethos and a "slavery" ethos by way of reintroducing the classical concepts of "free from coercion" and "self-sufficiency." Pertinent in this connection is his comment on how our technocracy tends to promote a slavery ethos by cultivating heteronomous conduct: "It has always been the case that the rulers try to imprison their fellowmen in cages made of ideas and passions. To this process of conditioning today's technocracy and technology have opened immense possibilities, so that the threat of a subtle enslavement of the human species becomes greater by the day. And now the question for us is this: Do these new barbaric modes possess the power to extinguish the love of freedom in man once and for all?" *The Crisis of Our Civilization* (1978), p. 271.

under way, situations like the one so vividly portrayed in Orwell's 1984, succeed in weakening the foundations of freedom. And in due course, even the rhetoric of democracy withers away until there are hardly any vestiges of the substance of freedom left to uplift one's image of human dignity.

Reacting to these imminent dangers, Papanoutsos' sense of urgency has issued in three recommendations, all of which embody the ethical precepts of humanism and the values of humanistic education. They are recommendations to his fellow Greeks but also meant to serve as guiding lines for any cultural and educational program as well as a more general political plan for survival:

(i) To value and sustain one's own culture and the viable traditions that define and enhance the particular character and physiognomy of the people, and do so with all due respect for the same of others.

(ii) To uphold their faith in the cooperative spirit of the ideals of humanism as shaped by the creative merging of the classical and Christian outlooks in their search for ways to establish universal peace.

(iii) To promote social solidarity and cultivate attitudes supportive of the goals of distributive justice.

For Papanoutsos there can be no compromise of the basic axiom of civilized life: justice in all expressions of social life and respect for the sacred right of all human beings to freedom and happiness. Having fully understood the implications of our postwar tensions, Papanoutsos missed no opportunity to underscore the immoral workings of military technocracies whose eventual clash can trigger nothing less than a global holocaust. If it is possible for the super-powers to act irresponsibly and destroy all life on earth, it should be equally possible for them to avert such action by moving in the opposite direction. But in order to promote the goal of universal peace our educational systems have to be strengthened not through pedantic lectures in the humanities but by transmitting to this and the on-coming generations the ideals of a humanistic *paideia*.

Practical as well as theoretical considerations led Papanoutsos to hold the application of his humanism inseparable from the pursuit of the democratic way of life. No compromises should be tolerated, for to ignore their implications is tantamount to undermining the conditions for the preservations of civilized life. On this principle, then, he insists, it becomes clear why it is that we cannot be free so long as we are subject to the threats of violent acts portending the destruction of defenseless individuals and nations. The ultimate justification of freedom lies in the pursuit and

18

promotion of justice for all, the powerful and the weak, in every expression of life and for the total society of all nations.

III. The Crisis of our Culture

As so many other brilliant commentators have noted in recent decades, Papanoutsos in his own way has underscored, and with a critical and penetrating eye, the gains as well as the debilitating effects which the modern developments have had on the quality of contemporary life. The question that has been repeatedly raised concerns the failure of the last few centuries of technological progress and intellectual refinements to bring the living generations of human beings in this century closer to the end which the modern era had so proudly declared to be mankind's noble end and destiny: fulfillment in freedom. Even the milder critics, and Papanoutsos being one of them, share a widespread conviction that our culture is in a state of crisis. At least this much may be admitted: since our culture is going through a state of crisis, a phase of real difficulty, to borrow an expression from medicine, the more stern observers take it to be one of impasse and therefore serious enough to pose a question of life and death. By combining what both groups are saying by way of diagnosis and prognosis, it would seem that the next stage in the unfolding of the crisis could be phrased by way of two sharply differing alternatives: either seek a solution through a thorough readjustment to the changes and challenges rooted in the problems of an altered yet manageable environment and complex system of social institutions; or surrender to the possibility of a radical transformation of this culture through hastened dissolution and assist in the selective absorption of the remaining healthy tissue into a new and essentially different one than the present.

We live in critical times because we continue to tolerate ambivalent attitudes and practices by bending the criteria of personal and social consistency, thus postponing and even blatantly avoiding to face the challenge to bring our conduct in line with the ideals we have inherited and to which we claim to be committed. The outcome of this discrepancy is the persistent paradox that has puzzled many a statesman and baffled most moral and political philosophers. Plainly stated, the paradox is this: we have made it possible to regard human autonomy the cornerstone of moral life, and the conception of freedom it entails the foundation of our public institutions; yet, we foster conditions that lead to doing violence or encourage the abuse of the principle of freedom when material advantages demand it. The factors which engender this paradox, while serving with remarkable efficacy certain types of interests, also function to make us insensitive to the spread of heteronomy. In presenting his point of view and discussing his analysis of the picture of humanity, Papanoutsos, as an eye-witness of his times, is as unswerving and direct in his evaluative disclosures as he is careful and objective in reporting his observations. He has focused on seven distinctive features which he believes define the paradoxical nature of our twentieth century. In brief outline they amount to the following:

1. *This has been a century of unprecedented violence.* The list of supporting facts is formidable: two world wars of massive proportions, two great social revolutions, the Russian and the Chinese, a number of bitter civil wars, particularly the ones in Spain, Greece and Ireland, numerous unsettling clashes in the Middle East, senseless destruction of life and property affecting millions of human beings due to expulsions and forced exchange of populations. Despite the frequent appeals to freedom, respect for tradition and national pride, neither the degrading of life nor the ruination of venerable cultural monuments could be stopped during the course of hostilities.

2. *This has been a century of spectacular scientific progress.* Major discoveries in all scientific fields and the ever-increasing applications of technical knowledge have brought profound changes in the social fabric of every nation. On the positive side, these developments have made it possible for larger numbers of consumers to have access to more leisure, and enabled industries to increase food production, provide fast transportation of persons and goods, quicken the conquest of space, expand mass communication systems, and revolutionize the storage and instant retrieval of vital information. Science has raised our expectations for the eventual alleviation of famine and poverty, the prevention of major catastrophies and the conquest of disease in the not too distant future. The feasibility of a shared international pool of scientific work is not an unrealistic dream. The obstacles exist, but they are due to non-scientific factors and interests.

3. *This has been a century of ever-expanding demands for general education.* The rise of democratic ways of government brought with them the demand to extend the benefits of learning to wider social groups. Thus the availability of education at advanced levels is no longer taken to be the prerogative of the privileged classes. Social reforms and the exigencies of technology made it mandatory to open up more and more fields of special learning to greater numbers of persons. The spreading of university education parallels the demand to meet the staffing of new professions and re-

spond to the need for wider participation in government and management. The educational process was greatly facilitated with the aid of the inexpensive products of mass communication technology. What is now being eliminated is not some elementary form of illiteracy but the obsolete economic conditions that made advanced training in the sciences and the industrial and fine arts tied to class, prestige and privilege.

4. *This has been a century of post-industrial economy and bureaucratization of public and private life.* The increasing dependency of both Eastern and Western nations on the modernized methods of production, finance, and distribution of goods to meet massive demands, has led to the adoption of novel patterns in the organization of post-industrial economy. [11] Their superior efficacy may be unquestionable, but the most disturbing outcome of this development is the surging of unplanned tensions and antinomies as well as novel forms of misery and subtle enslavement. Like the Industrial Revolution, the post-industrial economy has not been free from problems of mental health, stress situations, massive insecurity, an alarming rate of drug abuse and outbursts of violence to express social and political disillusionment. The infrastructure of government in many countries appears to be in a state of disarray. The frequent resorting to senseless crime and other types of destruction to combat the deeper causes of frustration, far from helping to replace the "diseased" order with a more humane one, have only led to more anarchy and the counter-measures of more authoritarian controls. It has now become evident that the grand expectation to see the efficient model of scientific rational planning transferred bodily over to the political sphere for the management of cultural and social affairs was but an idle dream. Social engineering has proved unable to advance itself to the level of political wisdom.

5. *This has been a century of revolution in sexual mores.* Much

---

[11] Papanoutsos distinguishes between two types of post-industrial patterns of economy: (a) the Western, which has worked out a new type of capitalism ranging in organizational operations from internal monopolies to multinationals, the latter enjoying relative autonomy by developing a *sui generis* technocracy; and (b) the Eastern, which has emerged with complexities of its own, controlled as it is by state authorities and political bureaucracy. However, he argues, neither pattern has successfully worked out solutions without after-effects that are free from the tendency to generate interferences with highly undesirable and counter-productive results: e.g., the streamlining of private and social life, disorders due to massive urbanization movements and other disintegrative trends that contribute to further the dislocation of the last connections between citizen and state. Among the most unpleasant consequences of the latter are the diverse type of anarchism and the rising rate of senseless crimes.

has been said in favor of the persistent efforts to introduce up-to-date information for the reshaping of sexual roles and relationships. However, the most positive gain of this movement is reflected mainly in the emancipation of women. The real loss, as yet not recognized as such, has been the increasing acceptance of substituting sexual gratification for love between the sexes. What has been retired in the process was not so much the "old mores," the removal of which still moves many to tears, but the meaning of the family unit. The home has ceased in many cases to provide the protective environment for the offspring nor is it conceived as the natural cove of parenthood. What the twentieth century has altered in the field of human sexuality is not so much progressive liberation from restrictive mores and stern regulations, although it has accomplished that much for a good number of individuals. Rather, it provided a basis for the theoretical justification of attitudes that can quickly graduate to licence, deviation and abuse without immediate arousal of guilt.

6. *This has been a century of radical artistic innovations.* Paralleling the information explosion is a rapid-fire type of creative breakthroughs in artistic technique, style and form, all pursued in response to the quest for aesthetic freedom. The great diversity of artistic works produced in this century with their widened band of innovative surprises expanded our aesthetic sensibility as much as it evoked a wealth of unsuspected emotional nuances. However, with the new waves of creativity and the recognition of the value of the cultural role of art, came the flooding of the market place and the release of confusing commentaries on the message of the visual and plastic arts, poetry and prose. Yet, the message itself, whenever it could issue forth with some degree of clarity, proved of no help to illumine the puzzles of the human condition. More often than not it added to the sense of anxiety and the feeling of a fading existence.

7. *This has been a century of diminishing democracy.* What has been perhaps the most baffling feature of the century is the sign of a converging of trends and movements directly or indirectly working against the preservation of the form of government that was heralded to be the crowning achievement of modern man. Chief among the practices that have compromised human freedom, are the rise of fascism and totalitarian governments, the ambivalent attitude of the established democracies toward such regimes, the yielding of our liberal ways to the pressures of technocracy in exchange for new forms of centralized authority, and the shift of the government's main concern from preserving political freedom to involvement in business.

When all these features are viewed together and their role in determining the quality of civilized life is assessed, one cannot help but sympathize with Papanoutsos' formulation of the paradox of our culture. He urges his reader to ask the burning question of how the human being, so qualitatively superior to the other animals, can succeed in consolidating scientific discoveries, coordinate production and effective management, and yet fail to master the forces within us that are responsible for so much rapacity, destruction and injustice.

Our century has no doubt earned the right to be recognized for its incomparable achievements in science and industry. Yet, its collective social record can hardly claim to have succeeded in doing the same in the domain of ethical amelioration. One is therefore inclined to conclude that the mind of man is no longer master of the fate of our culture. Hence the crisis of our civilization is a real one. And if there is a way out, Papanoutsos insists, it will be found neither through a renewed sense of self-pity for our sinful ways, nor by trying to secure peace through the balance of power and escalating the armament race. His general conclusion has the crispness of an epigram: "We have indeed made progress in this century but we have failed to be happy."

How, then, can we reconcile the steady rise of such evils as organized and senseless crime at the local and international levels, acts of genocide, disoriented imaginations, emotional emptiness and disillusionment, indifference and skepticism often bordering on cynical acceptance of fatalism, and increasing numbers of drug addicts, with our determination to unlock the remaining secrets of the universe? And more importantly, what are we to say about the living generations of human beings in view of the fact that collectively we have precipitated the crisis in the first place?

Papanoutsos has taken the position that the essence of culture is fundamentally mythical. Proceeding from this idea, he advances the interpretation that the manipulative and intellectual processes of contemporary man have tampered thoughtlessly with the entire mythical system and its modes of symbolism. We have disengaged and altered the quality of life that took centuries of cultural industriousness and creativity to build and integrate into a comprehensive outlook. He considers the following to be the dominant features of this system: a philosophy of right reason, the independence of religious consciousness, a view of viable government based on political liberalism, the conception that knowledge yields power, and an understanding of art as being a special case of erotic inspiration.

According to Papanoutsos, what took place during the last few centuries is that the critical powers of the cognitive life were pushed to the extreme, forcing thus the mind to adopt a continuous search for weaknesses. The process was carried out methodically and relentlessly for the sake of freeing our values and our institutions from the domination of all types of dogmatism. The outcome of this persistent effort was that the cutting knife of criticism became so sharp as to bleed the mythical substance of modern Western culture to death. More specifically, criticism *in extremis* denuded all our axiological constructions and frameworks from their mythical tissue. Thus, science surrendered willingly its hold on all immutable truths, ethics was deprived of its traditionally stable foundations, and art abandoned all vestiges of decency by using its license liberally to define its aims apart from the quest for beauty. Perhaps the most dangerous case of demythologizing was that of the state. By removing the mythical elements from its complex structure, the state lost in turn its basic social character and acquired a new and dominantly operational status within the framework of ideology. One of the immediate consequences was that the end of *eudaimonia* was jettisoned to make room for the emerging goal: how to pursue and secure power.

For Papanoutsos, the catalytic power of the methods of criticism in philosophy and the other fields of intellectual activity, originally aimed at the vigilant checking of traditional and new forms of dogmatism. But along with the refinement of critical tools also came the formation of a related habit as a way of viewing the human condition. The combination of the two created a strong trend of analysis that terminated in the technique of demythologizing the entire spectrum of cultural expressions. The difficulties that confront us now appear insurmountable not because they resist further analysis, but because they produce a feeling of utter helplessness that paralyzes our capacity to recover from the state of shock. Many of us cannot even decide whether the present crisis is one of "normal growth," like the one that attends the period of adolescence, or one that signals the arrival at an "ultimate impasse." The optimists are hoping for a healthier myth soon to arrive on the scene through some sort of cultural epiphany of a miraculous regeneration. The pessimists remain convinced that final chaos and perhaps a long period of utter darkness is about to cast its long shadow over our heads. After examining both sides of the debate, Papanoutsos cautioned that hope for a breakthrough lies in the direction of genuine changes in the existing social structures.

"Without a deep change in the structure of our system . . .

without first instituting another type of society, one that is different from *ours*, whether of the Eastern or the Western type, whether communist or capitalist, our sufferings are bound to continue and quite likely will become worse . . . We may not have the answer now, but we know one thing for certain and that is that we cannot go on living without hope."[12]

IV. The Critical Philosopher

In the Preface to his book, *Philosophical Problems*, Papanoutsos states the following on his own conception of the critical procedures of philosophical thinking:

> I have always called my way of viewing philosophical themes "critical philosophy" in order to signify the method I followed in my inquiries. The opening essay of this book, titled "The Critical Philosopher," explains what the term 'critical' means in my own case. It signifies self-imposed limits and disciplined thinking. It also means a determination neither to expound dogmatically nor impose arbitrarily any of my theses. Instead, it means that we are willing to subject our views to open discussion and careful examination while being ready to reject those that scrutiny shows to be false. This principle constitutes not only an intellectual but also a moral stance which few ever want to adopt and even fewer follow consistently . . . Real learning is not so much the amassing of reliable beliefs, however certain, but the assimilating of the lessons concerning the right method of how to arrive at such beliefs.[13]

It is instructive to follow Papanoutsos' analyses of philosophical systems and accounts of developments in the transformation of problems. But perhaps one of the most impressive discussions is that which deals with the crisis of our culture. A distinctive mark of Papanoutsos' approach and study of this complex problem is his remarkable spirit of detachment and balanced judgment. It offers a re-assurance that goes beyond the solace we expect to derive from statements of compassion when so many prophets of doom herald their disturbing messages. Papanoutsos' combination of objectivity and concern is related to his sustained practice and comprehension of the features of reasoned conduct that converge in the ideal of critical thinking. These traits are hallmarks of the human spirit, and have emerged with the conceptual contributions of a long line of thinkers in the intellectual traditions of the West, reaching back to the days of early Greek philosophy. His version of what it is to be a critical philosopher, how to

---

[12] *The Crisis of Our Civilization* (1978), pp. 46–47.
[13] *Philosophical Problems* (1963), p. 8.

function critically in response to the quest for truth and values, is neither a description of his own struggles and attainments nor the finished picture of an actual historical period. Rather, it is offered as an ideal summarizing and expressing what our own cultural and critical humanism sets forth as a funded source of guidance and a model worthy of emulation. Even if all we can personally do is approximate it, this ideal of the critical philosopher is drawn with remarkable detachedness and maintains its appeal despite the social turmoil, political convulsions and cultural changes that have rocked our century.

In a way, Papanoutsos' version of the critical thinker reminds us of the great Hellenistic portraits of the wise man, of the visions of Epicurus, Zeno, Marcus Aurelius, and their admirable original, the dialectical man in Plato's *Republic*. Yet Papanoutsos, the dedicated educator, views the critical outlook as being more than an ideal embodied only in rare occasions in the conduct of a handful of extraordinary thinkers in the intellectual and scientific tradition of the West. He is fully convinced that democracy, through the offices of education, can render what has hitherto been an infrequently traveled path into a wide and well paved avenue, by making critical intelligence a public good and an openly pursued social ethos. This makes Papanoutsos a supporter of intellectual solutions, an advocate of educational reforms, and a firm believer in the practical value of the theoretical virtues, redefined once again to meet the demands of our own historical conditions. He is fully aware of how often even whole generations fail to embody any ideal, and more so the ideal of philosophical and critical intelligence, especially since the conditions that can bring it about depend on the pressence of freedom of expression, something few periods of history have succeeded in sustaining long enough to make a difference in the quality of public life. Yet he misses no opportunity to recommend its vitality and defend it as the best means to solve the problems of humanity. He writes:

> I personally believe that the genuine type of philosophical thought, which is also consistent with its own principles, presupposes a definite kind of intelligence, and first of all a definite ethos which is at once an intellectual program and an ethical stance. The acquisition of this perspective is interwoven with a definite type of temperament, one that requires a special type of education — a combination of factors that is rather rare, to be sure. [14]

It would be helpful to pause briefly at this point to present in bare outline the distinctive features which according to Papanoutsos

---

[14] *Philosophical Problems* (1963), p. 12.

delineate the outlook of the critical philosopher. First and foremost is the passion for knowledge, one that in its uncompromising exercise of refutation is always moving beyond opinion, always searching for reliable and warranted beliefs. It is what makes the philosopher the knower *par excellence.* But he is also a person with a deep sense of responsibility, one whose love of fellow human beings is so strong and enlightened as to display the highest degree of compassionate understanding. It is this refinement of reasoned sentiment that makes the philosopher a lover of both wisdom and humanity, one who sits in judgment of ideas and theories, never of human beings. The critical thinker is not a dogmatist when he must pass judgment, unlike most people whose claim to tolerance never goes beyond pretension, while failure to practice it is most frequently the rule. The fact remains that only the dogmatist identifies the person with the ideas he holds; and when he has to cope with the source of what he considers to be a nuissance, he unflinchingly proceeds to control adverse ideas by destroying their bearer. This model of dogmatic conduct has served as the rule for most cases of historically influential actions and explains why so many persecutions, religious and political, and other social calamities have stained the pages of history by spilling the blood of the innocent with the fanatical determination only the self-righteous possess. The type of dogmatism that breeds intolerance is justly regarded as most abhorrent to the temper of the philosophical mind.

The ethos of the critical philosopher is a genuine paradigm of prudence, self-control and self-discipline. It is the ethos we associate with persons forever unwilling to surrender their freedom or diminish their devotion to this ideal. Paramount to this type of conduct is the continuous display of philosophical courage, a determination to follow one's convictions wherever they may lead and fully prepared to accept with unwavering equanimity all unpleasant consequences, from social disapproval and loneliness to bitter denouncement and exile. The philosopher has a duty to remain above ideologies, parties and all idols of the day. Thus the ethos that emerges through the steady practice of these features carries with it the demand that one can never compromise the commitment to reason nor cheapen the quality of life through wasteful undertakings. It also demands approval of only such acts as can sustain our self-respect while contributing to the same of others, doing justice to our humanity and by devoting our energies to the rejuvenation of our culture and the preservation of our attested values.

The biographer of Papanoutsos will no doubt be interested in correlating the aforementioned traits of the critical thinker to the ways in which Papanoutsos himself essayed to embody them in his own life and work. My own assignment in writing this essay has a different focus. It is deliberately limited to a discussion of his own understanding of the philosophical tasks he set out to meet when examining the complex problems of our century and their historical antecedents. What stands out rather sharply is the construction of his response through the close study of the two periods of enlightenment, the classical and the modern, which from the very start had engaged his attention. Some of his best writings were done in response to the need to examine the implications of this dual loyalty and to tracing their functional role in the contemporary scene.

It is necessary at this point to make a comment or two on the philosophical character of the two enlightenment movements before raising the issue of Papanoutsos' dual loyalty and its relation to his reflections on the contemporary crisis. By viewing the classical enlightenment as tied to the expanding pursuits characteristic of a persistent inquiry given to exploring and mapping the many ways of being, in contrast to the modern enlightenment which forced into the open the experimentalism that came with the passion to solve every epistemological issue regarding the limits and scope of knowledge, we are better prepared to accept the fact that each movement had its own distinct character and orientation. It would therefore be idle groping to look for a one-to-one correspondence or hope to discern a convergence of ideals in two significantly different outbursts of intellectual activity. Furthermore, it would likewise be a mistake to say that the respective humanisms of the two enlightenments coincide in the sets of values they sought to promote and defend. Papanoutsos has clearly understood all this and has contributed through his own writings to a fuller understanding of the divergent character that sets them apart yet renders them the greatest expressions of the same quest for an adequate humanism.

On the basis of these clarifications we may now proceed to mention the central issue that will be pursued in more detail in the next section. The main point here is that the relentlessly critical spirit of the modern enlightenment, as Papanoutsos has repeatedly emphasized, has contributed in no small measure to the making of the forces that created the impasse of our century. And did so mainly by paving the way for the process of demythologizing every aspect of the culture it sought to enrich, refine and understand. In this respect the classical enlightenment was no different, for the task was not only comparable but also the concern proved to be equally if not more intense. The catalytic process of demythologizing in both cases ended in a situation of institutional crisis which in turn undermined the great promise of a humanist culture. New waves of skepticism and irrationalism moved in from different directions and threatened to carry the day, and for a while they did exactly that.

The contemporary crisis, as Papanoutsos sees it, poses an ethical problem of considerable magnitude and takes the form of a dilemma. Since the need to find an exit can no longer be ignored, there are only two directions opening up for us to follow: either seek to bring about a cultural rejuvenation through a renaissance solution, or proceed with an attitude of radical defiance, along the lines Nietzsche suggested and in this century the poet Nikos Kazantzakis worked out in his epic poem, *The Odyssey: A Modern Sequel*, for the transvaluation of all values. The first alternative leaves undecided the role of classical humanism in effecting the new; the second makes it clear that its jettisoning becomes inevitable.

Papanoutsos' writings show that he is extremely sensitive to the implications of either of the above alternatives. His genuine concern for what may take place as we prepare for the next chapter in the history of the Western mind creates a feeling of deep agony over the survival of his own heritage, the fate of the cultural memory of thousands of years and its credentials of perennial significance. To this we must add the tantalizing prospect of an equally dark future for the intellectual monuments that comprise the European experience and heritage. His avowed commitment is such that cannot under any circumstances turn him into an advocate of radical transformations. Were this to become the only course of action to meet the crisis, it would herald the eventual demise of his own historical and cultural foundations.

These considerations do more than merely serve to outline the drama of the contemporary cultural crisis. They also determine the stance of persons who like E. P. Papanoutsos, have been courageous enough to defend the tradition of critical humanism and raise their voice to demand a central place for the role of reason in the formation of the forces that are shaping the alternatives we need to face the future. The purpose of the last section of this essay is to present the case of E. P. Papanoutsos.

V. The Case of E. P. Papanoutsos

Papanoutsos as philosopher and educator, modern Greek and Western European, citizen and humanist, fits well in the tradition of the modern Enlightenment, as a follower and its brilliant, yet loyal, critic. Fully aware of the merits of the classical heritage, he also came to regard himself indebted to the modern modes of thought. In fact, it was to the lessons and experiences of the modern that he turned regularly for intellectual guidance and ideas to meet the demands for the educational reforms Greece needed in this century to close the cultural gap between itself and the Western European countries. One needs to remember at this point that Greece was still a province of the Ottoman empire when eighteenth and early nineteenth century Europe was formulating and then fighting to implement the social and political ideas of the Enlightenment. When Byron came to what was then unliberated Greece for his second and last visit in 1823, he brought with him the poetic visions of romantic politics and less of the toughness of statesmanship which the practical leaders of the Enlightenment had shown in action. In a way, it was the spirit of Byron that determined the climate of opinion that was to prevail in that small parcel of what is traditionally Grecian land that was turned into an independent state and whose destiny was to be ruled by two kings who were former princes of the royal houses of Bavaria the first, and Denmark, the second. With the dawn of the twentieth century, Greece had solved no basic problems at all and had succeeded only in stirring its political and literary imagination by listening to the last fainting spells of a despirited Romanticism. Greece had missed the lessons of the Enlightenment, just as it had the misfortune not to profit from the experience of the Renaissance, to the occurrence of which it had contributed in no small measure through the flight of its scholars and philosophers to the West.

Responding to the urgent needs of his people, Papanoutsos did what was at once practical and necessary. He prepared himself for the tasks of education by assimilating the modern European experience as expressed in its arts and letters, its democratic ideals of political liberalism, its theories of justice and freedom, and particularly its faith in an education founded on the humanistic and critical philosophies of the Enlightenment. At the same time he had to face the difficulties of assessing the bitter realities of Greece in the aftermath of the First World War — something he had to do once again some twenty-five years later in the wake of the withdrawal of the Nazi occupation forces and the chaos that followed the civil strife of December 1944. When Papanoutsos turned twenty, none of the pressing national issues had been resolved; millions of unredeemed Greeks were still living in traditionally Greek lands under the Turks, while widespread illiteracy continued to aggravate the conditions of poverty in a sub-standard type of agricultural country ruled through the alliance between a bureaucratic hierarchy and a powerful merchant class using paternalistic practices in politics, the courts of law and higher education. It was only one year after Papanoutsos had published his first philosophical essay that his country suffered its first major setback in this century: the holocaust of the Greek population in Thrace and Asia Minor in 1922.

Papanoutsos was among the first to realize that recovery from the wounds of the war also called for new ideas, new programs and drastic reforms, especially in the system of education. He understood that the lessons of the Enlightenment were still valid for Greece, but their applicability depended not so much on passive inculcation of high-sounding conceptual schemes, but a determination to introduce the anti-dogmatic spirit of criticism for a thorough re-evaluation of national aspirations and wasteful institutional practices. Many of the conflicting elements in the total situation his generation had to understand and cope with were deeply imbedded in issues surfacing through the great controversy over the problem of recognizing the spoken language, the "demotic" as it is still called, "the language of the people," as an adequate cultural tool. However, behind this major controversy lurked another, even more divisive one, a *sui generis* battle between the ancients and the moderns, which in the case of modern Greece summarized the crucial problem of how to ensure national survival, identity and continuity. In the course of events, Papanoutsos offered a solution of his own for at least part of the problem. He reached it by siding first with the progressive forces that had been fighting to defend the adequacy of the demotic and its suitability to serve the letters and the sciences, and then later by gradually reworking the thesis of critical humanism into a broader philosophical view that could embrace the lasting ideas of classical Greek philosophy, the living social message of Christianity, and the political insights of the modern Enlightenment. It was a solution which in its initial stage and in all its subsequent elaborations was founded on the concept of freedom as the human condition: that freedom is both a right and a duty.

Papanoutsos' search for a way to resolve the conflict between the ancients and the moderns, or to put it differently, the problem of preserving and projecting the creative aspects of the classical through the modes of modern consciousness, led to a systematic study of the history of ethics, philosophy of art and culture, and the foundations of education. It was precisely this path of inquiry and this sequence of concerns that strengthened Papanoutsos'

31

confidence in the relevance of the Enlightenment to the contemporary scene in general. His assigning of priority to the practical value of the modern critical theories of mind brought with it not only the opening up of new opportunities for fresh investigations, but more importantly it generated a life-long interest in the modern interpretations of human consciousness, the first installments of which appeared in the themes of *The Trilogy of the Mind: Art, Ethics, Science,* in 1928, and then the special volumes, *About Art* (1930), *About Ethics* (1932), and *About Science* (1937). In line with this development, Papanoutsos did more than engage the results of recent epistemological investigations to study the creative domains of the mind. He contributed to the furtherance of the movement in significant ways; first through his critical observations for its methodological refinement; and then more systematically by illuminating a wider range of practical issues.

This emphasis on modern epistemology, when viewed in its historical setting, carries with it a negative pronouncement on another philosophical area: metaphysics. It was explicitly worked out in the writings of David Hume and then found its definitive justification in Kant's first great *Critique.* By questioning the possibility of metaphysics, the epistemologists of the eighteenth century performed the most painful operation of the philosophical body of the tradition that had started with the Greeks: the claim to know Being. Man's faith in his ability and desire to know Being, to explore the secrets of reality and lay bare the isomorphic relationships that tie together logical principles and cosmic structures, had miraculously survived all skeptical attacks down to the end of the seventeenth century. The eighteenth century turned a new leaf in the history of the study of the mind and its products. For the future of metaphysics the coming of the eighteenth century marked the opening phase in what proved to be a series of masterworks in destructive criticism. The catalytic process was set in irreversible motion like an ever-expanding vortex destined to engulf in its powerful turns and twists one by one all the metaphysical truths about nature, man and his values.[15]

The Greeks were convinced that the quest they had started rested securely on a firm foundation, and hence it provided the same accommodations for reason and for being. So strong was this belief that even the great intellectual revolution of the sophistic

---

[15] See *Philosophy and Paideia* (1958), pp. 218–35. This section offers a detailed discussion of the eighteenth century and its antecedents. The main features of the Enlightenment are identified as (i) the celebration of right reason, (ii) deism and natural religion, (iii) faith in the freedom of thought, and (iv) strong desire for social emancipation and political rights.

movement could not shake their confidence. *Logos* as reason never acquired the power to build a wall between man and nature. Hence, their critiques of the origins and limits of knowledge, and, to be more precise, of *logos,* never reached the point of declaring the cognitive structures of the theoretical life open to the charge of metaphysical dogmatism. What the Greeks insisted they were talking about, when they were not fighting among themselves, was always some real aspect of being. And this was not a conclusion; it was the major premise or a first principle, so to speak. It was a view so unlike what the eighteenth century critical inquiries into the nature and limits of knowledge were allowed to establish as the object of science. The modern verdict was taken to be an irrevocable conclusion, and was interpreted in many quarters to have announced the burial of the ontological quest. It appeared to many that the modern Enlightenment had completed what its ancient counterpart could not for lack of enough critical self-consciousness.

The post-classical adventures of the branch of philosophy that later on became known as "metaphysics," when the religious concern with its own quests and questions altered, transformed, and determined its subject-matter and affected the conception of its method, is another story. However, the adventures of metaphysics and what this enterprise stood for by the time the critical minds of the Enlightenment sought to investigate it as a province of philosophy, do form an important part of the historical background needed for the fuller understanding of Papanoutsos' case, especially his dual loyalty. How much of the field of metaphysics which became the target of Hume's and Kant's attacks was Greek in origin and how much non-Greek was not brought up for careful discussion. The foremost issue was the claim that had been made in the name of metaphysics to know reality. Nor did it matter to the critical epistemologists what 'reality' stood for, whether the natural world of the Greeks, the spiritual entities of the Neopythagoreans and the Neoplatonists, or the diverse supernatrual realms of the religious thinkers of the Christian and the other faiths. All conceptions of reality, classical medieval and that of the Renaissance humanists, had finally come up for scrutiny; in fact, the most thorough scrutiny in the intellectual history of the Western world since the days of Socrates, Plato and Aristotle.

When epistemology brushed all metaphysical claims aside, it did so without making any exceptions. All realities, Greek or otherwise, fell by the wayside after Kant finished his "Copernican revolution" in the field of knowledge. The critical mind had made its case for the dismissal of the theological, cosmological, and moral absolute verities from the domain of meaningful inquiry. As the contributions of the Enlightenment continued to grow by working out the implications they had for the arts and the sciences, the climate for metaphysical speculation grew less and less favorable.

What was not immediately understood then, and even later remained a moot question, was that the opposition between epistemology and metaphysics was in essence a quarrel between the modern, on the one hand, and the medieval and its value components, on the other, that had found their way into the scientific and artistic visions of the Renaissance, and not a clash between the modern and the classical. The victor of the confrontation between the old and the new was the critical spirit of philosophy embodied fully in the epistemological pursuit. The critical theory of knowledge to which it gave rise succeeded in establishing the tradition of the new. E. P. Papanoutsos, like most modern and contemporary thinkers, had to work within this tradition and add to it. The most valuable contributions came from those thinkers who understood that the lessons of the Enlightenment called for extending the critical quest to include a thorough examination of the assumptions each generation of thinkers was making when seeking to correlate theory and practice. One of the reservations Papanoutsos formulated in the course of his analyses was that the critical mind over-extended itself and ended in an intellectual *hubris.* The analytic mind became a catalytic force threatening to unbraid the very culture it had labored to take the place of the theocratic conception that receded with the coming of the Renaissance.

As a critic of the critical mind, Papanoutsos identified the catalytic side as being responsible for bringing about in this century the destruction of myth, "the essence of culture." But his is mainly a reservation that calls to question, and correctly so, the practical consequences of the intellectual movement. It is important to introduce at this point the theoretical side of the issue: the relationship between the quest for knowledge and the quest for being. The question now becomes: is there a point to saying that it was incumbent upon Papanoutsos as a modern Greek to assign a place in his philosophy for the classical quest for being? His own cultural humanism is admittedly rooted in the critical spirit of the Enlightenment, which in turn remained dependent in its initial and subsequent developments on the advancements of critiques that gave primacy to the problem of knowledge over the ontological approach to nature and human nature. Is it then the case that

Papanoutsos' humanism must surrender the classical outlook on life and philosophy in order to comply with the primacy of the epistemological demands of the modern?

The questions concerning the case of E. P. Papanoutsos takes on additional seriousness because of two *desiderata* he has identified in his own studies of the contemporary crisis. In order to cope with the profound difficulties of the present predicament and avoid the further collapse of our institutions, we need first a strong antidote to *hubris,* and secondly to discover the way to neutralize the effects of demythologizing which the catalytic processes aid and abet. It is quite likely that neither can be done unless we can find a *modus operandi* to create conditions for the co-existence of the classical and the modern. We need to build a framework to encompass within it the classical and the modern in a synthesis that would be immune to the various philosophical dichotomies, such as the split that forces us to choose between the quests of epistemology and ontology as if these were mutually exclusive interests. In the absence of such a *modus operandi* we have to make do with a *modus vivendi* which is burdened with an anthropocentric humanism that views the natural world not as the reality which contains man and his works, but as one that can be understood only when placed within the mind to become "known" in accordance with the human schemes of cognition.

The case of Papanoutsos is a crucial one because it forces into the open one of the most pressing issues of our times: how to define and determine humanity's authentic place in the world that sustains us. Stated in a different way, the issue becomes this: is it at all possible to do justice to ourselves and our fellow human beings by relying mainly on the conviction that the only warranted beliefs about ourselves and what we call "reality" we can ultimately trust are those that are certified in the mental laboratories of our critical epistemologies? More than ever before it has now become obvious that, as a result, we have been putting the universe into our heads, thereby reversing the natural order of ordinary perception in order to satisfy the formulas of extraordinary conception. The road from this point to the diverse and often extreme modern subjectivisms in ethics, politics, aesthetics and education, is but an open highway. The pitfalls become visible to the travelers only after they have fallen victims and can no longer free themselves from the inflictions of self-entrapment. It is not an unfair characterization to say that the situation we call "the contemporary crisis" is in fact part of the most engaging cultural labyrinth that was ever devised throughout the few thousand years of our history.

One could also say — although this is but a personal conviction — that we are presently dealing with a mental and technological labyrinth with a built-in capacity to discredit all the products of its myth-making operations, except itself. The most intriguing feature of this labyrinth is that it has turned itself into the most persuasive of all other historical and bio-political myths. As such it constitutes the protective cocoon inside of which the creative mind spins the subtle yarn of modern consciousness. Yet, we are comfortably convinced that our times are so intensely critical as to be able to discern and dispell sooner rather than later all myths and all ideologies. We are the brave demythologizers. At the heart of our self-reliance is the belief that learning, technological expertise and epistemic sharpness have rendered us so astutely critical as to act with dispatch to excise from our body of beliefs even the most timid sproutings of a myth. Now that we have grounds to say with confidence that we know all that is to be known about the limits of cognition and criteria of warranted beliefs, there is no chance of letting new myths find their way into the fabric of destilled experience.

Papanoutsos sometimes gives the impression that the process of catalysis in our century has completed by now its task of demythologizing. Yet there seem to be at least one grand myth, however bad in its construction and clever in its manner of disguise, which was left untouched by the process of demythologizing in the twentieth century. It is the myth of the subjective labyrinth, one which sustains itself through the ever-deepening conviction that the life-line of our culture runs only through the constantly refineable methods of construction and production of our cognitive projections. The logic of the myth itself requires that the Labyrinth and the Minotaur be regarded as one and the same thing. With the fusion of the two, a self-deceiving intolerance of myth-making passes for logical integrity while cognitive self-righteousness declares itself immune to the deceptions of ontic transcendence. However, the resulting fusion causes the Labyrinth to lose its power to generate significance, and finally it emerges as nothing but the symbol of a cultural Mausoleum, one for each living-dead it contains in its dark chambers. As a monument, it is the crowning work of the genius of our century. Papanoutsos, expresses the same point differently, and is no less accurate in his diagnosis:

> With the arrival of the twentieth century, the denuding of the world of its magic, a process which started three hundred years ago, seems to be approaching its completion. Science, while succeeding in its goals, has dissolved all mystery, and technics is now being ushered

in to replace the sense of miracle. A new phase of our history has opened before us, a new page in human history is being written. [16]

In light of the preceding remarks, I want to emphasize two points:

1. The dominance of the epistemological quest in modern philosophy and the subsequent discrediting of ontology. The case of Papanoutsos is no exception, but his is a peculiar one in that his commitment to the modern Enlightenment required a painful decision which in turn, led to weighing the consequences of jettisoning a valuable part of his heritage, i.e., classical ontology.

2. The rise of epistemology had significant cultural implications not only in lending support to the forces that combined to further the objectives of a technologically oriented society. It also contributed immensely toward shifting the center of gravity in the domain of practical reason. A careful reading of the works of Papanoutsos shows that despite his direct involvement in public issues and the politics of educational reforms, his theoretical work has been carried out mainly in the field of ethics. Somehow, the concept of individual consciousness, in its ethical rather than its political expression, is what was brought in for detailed examination. Generally speaking, his is a critical humanism, but in its orientation and concern it is ethical rather than political. When in his later writings he focused his attention on the problem of the contemporary crisis, he showed that the demythologizing of the state was fraught with bad omens. And though he regretted the demise of the political consciousness of the ancient Greeks, he has produced no theoretical statement to argue its priority over the ethical consciousness of the individual.

Here again, the case of Papanoutsos is one which tests the dual alliance of the modern Greek modality of cultural adjustment in response to the modern. He develops and defends a critical humanism, in line with the spirit which has sustained modern epistemology — the spirit of individual consciousness — and in doing so, his vote of confidence is cast in favor of the modern. Thus ethics emerges not as a chapter in politics, as in Aristotle, but as a theoretical discipline which inquires into the form of virtue, though not the historically practiced patterns of moral excellence. But, insofar as ethics overlaps with the philosophy of culture, ethics inquires into the implications which the concepts of freedom and moral consciousness have for critical humanism. In essence Papanoutsos has followed the path of the modern.

---

[16] *Ibid.*, p. 235. The suggestion is that technics is presently functioning as a surrogate myth, serving in this capacity to replace "the miraculous."

There, again, we witness an inversion of the classical, but not its denial. Politics, like ontology, is not jettisoned; it is discovered through the enlargement of self in its public involvement.

It would be unfair to push the point further. The case of Papanoutsos' critical humanism is basically modern — and in the last analysis, modern Greek. It lays the foundations for a creative rapprochement between the classical and the modern. The crucial test of its cultural usefulness, and, we may add, its political importance, lies in its power to follow what may well be the lost thread of Ariadne and discover the exit out of the impasse of our crisis; it suggests the negation of the sterile myth of the modern Labyrinth.

As a student of Papanoutsos' philosophy, I have found it impossible to conclude that this brilliant modern Greek has assimilated the European Enlightenment in all its creative moments only to compromise at the end the significance and promise his own heritage still holds for humanity. Papanoutsos embraced neither easy nor soothing solutions. Just as his intensive analyses of the problem of knowledge lead to a view which re-opens the road for a fresh look at the problem of being, so does his critical humanism as a philosophy of culture hold a definite promise for a dynamic and constructive approach to the political problem that lies at the heart of the crisis of our culture. In both instances, Papanoutsos works through the modern in order to address the grand issues of our time, but with a sharp eye for the lessons of history and, above all, the history of philosophy.

There is another side to the case of Papanoutsos which suggests his intimacy with the creative quality of his heritage. The only symbol I can think of as being most appropriate to this side of his thought is the Phoenix, the mythical bird which rises from its own ashes.

It may well be that the discovery of the exit allowing us to put an end to the present crisis may come only through a series of self-transformations, a series of re-births from the ashes of our own predicaments. After all, every competent historian of culture knows that the European mind is not a negation of the classical heritage; in the last analysis, it is but a different and later phase in the active life of the same entity: human consciousness. Like all phases of the human condition, the modern was able to solve certain problems while it created some of its own. Like the other preceding phases, it too has its own credentials of historical authenticity and its own style. Sometimes, the problems outpace the solutions, and when the burdens reach the point of saturation, we witness the signs of a cultural dead-end. This, in turn, signals the time for another transformation, another creative outburst of the human condition. The same human resourcefulness readies itself for the new tasks. Out of its present ashes once again the Phoenix is re-born . . .

I may have read into the case of Papanoutsos more than he may want to accept. But at least I hope I have not misunderstood his philosophy of culture. My reading aside, the case of Papanoutsos is not only unusual; it is also an admirable one. It summarizes the issues and sharpens the problems that one must face when assigning to the classical tradition a place in the urgencies of the contemporary. Seen as a personal achievement, it is a model of philosophical self-consciousness and self-engagement in the creative pursuits of the practical life. But the broader, the *political*, significance of the case of Papanoutsos can be more adequately grasped when seen as a case of the mind searching for the exit after seeing the most terrifying prospects of the modern Labyrinth. The key concept in the case of Papanoutsos is that of *the critical philosopher*, the torch-bearer of critical humanism seeking to transmute the duty to freedom as an ethical principle, into a public act as the foundation for a political philosophy of the future. Some may find this concept worthy of emulation; others may consider it a source of comfort. Whatever its use, or its appeal, it is so carefully delineated as to serve its main function well: a model of heightened human self-consciousness at its best.

In another context, that of hopefulness, the case of Papanoutsos offers good reasons why total cultural bankruptcy is not within the realm of the possible. For the collective body of free human beings no cultural malady ever becomes fatal, no matter what the dimensions of violence. In holding this conviction, Papanoutsos confirms his affinity with Plato and Aristotle. There is something about humanity that is genuinely "deathless" and "indestructible." It is the inalienable right to freedom. So long as · there is at least one human being who bears it well and does it justice, the creative flame will not be extinguished. In due course the burning flames will turn all impurities into ashes, and there from the ashes the Phoenix is sure to stir again ready for its next rebirth.

John P. Anton
Emory University

SUPPLEMENT

THE MAJOR WORKS OF
EVANGELOS P. PAPANOUTSOS

(Six Decades of Literary Activity)

1921 THE QUESTION OF THE FREEDOM OF WILL
1924 THE PHILOSOPHY OF HENRI BERGSON. Lecture
1924 PRAGMATISM OR HUMANISM. ELABORATION AND
CRITICISM OF THE THEORIES OF A GREAT
CURRENT OF CONTEMPORARY PHILOSOPHY
1924 THE FREEDOM OF WILL (SECOND THOUGHTS)
1927 DAS RELIGIÖSE ERLEBEN BEI PLATON (Greek
edition, 1971)
1927 INTRODUCTION TO THE PHILOSOPHY OF
RELIGION
1928 THE TRILOGY OF THE MIND: ART, ETHICS,
SCIENCE
1930 ABOUT ART
1932 ABOUT ETHICS
1937 ABOUT SCIENCE
1939 PLATO'S PHAEDO. Ancient text. Introduction,
translation, notes
1940 ELEMENTS OF PSYCHOLOGY
1948 THE WORLD OF THE MIND. Vol. I: AESTHETICS
1949 THE WORLD OF THE MIND. Vol. II: ETHICS
1949 PALAMAS-CAVAFY-SIKELIANOS. Three studies (new
edition, 1955)
1950 EPHEMERA
1953 LA CATHARSIS DES PASSIONS D'APRÈS ARISTOTE
1953 MODERN GREEK PHILOSOPHY. Vol. I (BASIC
LIBRARY, Vol. 35)
1954 THE WORLD OF THE MIND. Vol. III: THE
FOUNDATIONS OF KNOWLEDGE (English edition,
1968)
1956 MODERN GREEK PHILOSOPHY. Vol. II (BASIC
LIBRARY, Vol. 36)
1956 MODERN GREEK CRITICISM. With I. M.
Panayotopoulos and Dion. Zakythinos (BASIC LIBRARY,
Vol. 42)

ΕΡΓΑ ΤΟΥ ΕΥΑΓΓΕΛΟΥ Π. ΠΑΠΑΝΟΥΤΣΟΥ

('Εξήντα Χρόνια)